Listening to Both Sides

CIVIC VIRTUES

Mindy Huffman

CIVICS FOR THE REAL WORLD™

Rosen Classroom™

We are planning a class trip.
Where should our class go?

Sara thinks we should go to the zoo. Bryan thinks we should visit a farm.

Our teacher asks Bryan and Sara to share their ideas. Our class will listen to both sides.

Sara says the zoo has more animals. Our class will learn more there.

Bryan says the farm has animals, too. There are chickens, cows, and sheep.

Sara says there is more to do at the zoo. We could pet a snake or feed a parrot.

Bryan says there are things to do on the farm, too. We could pick beans or brush a horse.

Sara says our class could ride the zoo train. We could see all the animals faster.

Bryan says our class could go on a hayride. A tractor would drive us around the farm.

The zoo wins! Sara and Bryan shake hands. It was good to listen to both sides.

WORDS TO KNOW

beans

hayride

parrot

tractor